IF YOU LOVE THEM
LEAVE THEM
LISTS

CATHERINE RAHAL
WENDY MOENIG

If You Love Them, Leave Them Lists!
A Guide to Navigate Difficult Conversations and Organize Your Affairs

1st edition May 2021
2nd edition October 2021

3rd edition July 2022
Published by catherinerahal.com

Cover and Interior Design: Wendy Moenig
Editor: Richard Tardif
Photography: Photos of Wendy Moenig and Catherine Rahal
by Robin Andrew, Unposed Photography, Carleton Place, ON
Collaboration: Wendy Moenig

Disclaimer

This book contains the ideas and opinions of its author. The intention of this book is to provide information, helpful content, and motivation to readers about the subjects addressed. Although every precaution has been taken to verify the accuracy of the information contained herein, the author and publisher assume no responsibility for any errors or omissions. The intent of this author is only to offer suggestions to help the reader in the quest for organizing their personal affairs. The author and publisher urge readers to seek professional legal counsel and appropriate expert advice.

No warranties or guarantees are expressed or implied by the author's choice to include any of the content in this volume. The author shall not be liable for any physical, psychological, emotional, financial, or commercial damages, including, but not limited to, special, incidental, consequential, or other damages. The reader is responsible for their own choices, actions, and results.

ISBN: 978-1-7781988-0-9

IF YOU LOVE THEM

LEAVE THEM
LISTS

Dedication

This book is dedicated to
my sons, Jamal and Hakim, and their late father, Salah-Eddine.

Table of Contents

Introduction

When my husband died in a 1983 commercial airline accident, litigation followed and eventually, a substantial financial settlement. I was young — only 33 — too naive and trusting (not to mention traumatized); I put my faith in the wrong person and lost my proverbial shirt. That was the catalyst for becoming a personal financial advisor in 1991, starting in life insurance and moving quickly into investments. I enjoyed over 25 years of providing advice to people, with the guiding principle that no client of mine should ever have to suffer financially as I did.

I also tried to make easier the difficult conversations we tend to avoid, those involving insurance, disability, old age, and death. It has always surprised me how many people do not want to discuss life insurance or making a will. No one wants to think about mortality, but it comes to us all. Sorting out our wishes in the event of incapacity or death will be a lot easier for our representatives if they have the necessary information at hand.

When we reach a certain age, our conversations are laced with tales of our parents having health and memory issues, caregiver woes, and how, as adult children, we are simultaneously managing childcare and parent care while working full time, handling our own health issues, and more. There is no magic wand to help us manage it all. Many of the decisions we need to make in old age are too often made in crisis mode, frequently after a health event or accident (like a fall), when it becomes clear that living alone becomes a risky option.

Many of us are convinced we will die at home. If I had a dollar for every time someone has said to me, "I am leaving this house feet first," I'd have a nice little nest egg. Not all of us are lucky enough to control those last few years.

I have served as power of attorney, mandatary, and executor for an old friend who had dementia. That experience left me with an enormous amount of respect for those people who work as caregivers, powers of attorney, and mandataries/health proxies for us when we can no longer competently care for ourselves.

In the last year of my father's life, my mother categorically forbade me to discuss anything estate or death-related with him. After his death, I forced the issue with her, and it did help. When I began to notice signs of her cognitive decline:

- I made sure her will and power of attorney documents were up to date — while she was still legally able to sign.

- I began to research residences since she could no longer live alone.

- I had the house evaluated as she was house-rich and cash-poor — you cannot pay a caregiver with pieces of the physical house.

- And I surreptitiously recorded the after-meal conversations where she recounted her life as a half-Jewish person in Berlin before, during, and after the war. We have a historical legacy to leave, and children often don't think to ask until it is too late. If you have stories to tell, record them.

And just because I have some idea of what needs to be considered, it doesn't mean my family is in sync with me. My children tolerate my ramblings, but I still have to put it all on paper.

Through personal experiences and what I have learned from clients, I have seen that many of us plan for marriage, houses, children, vacations, retirement — everything except old age. We need to change that. We can't plan for every eventuality, but we can set guidelines for our wishes. We can record the information our designated representatives will need to act in our stead, whether we are incapacitated or have left the living behind. And it doesn't hurt to check out a few residences — even if you never end up in one.

PART ONE

Why this book?

Why this book?

One of the biggest fears most of us share is losing control of our bodies and minds as we age. Our bodies betray us, and our minds don't always stay as sharp as we'd like. A legacy notebook is a way to exert some control over how the last part of your life will unfold. Having guidelines in place will enable your representatives to reach out to the right people to find help and can go a long way towards reducing the stress generated when life throws your world into crisis mode.

Many of us do, eventually, put insurance and wills in place, as well as powers of attorney*, and mandates or healthcare/financial proxies in the event of incapacity, but there is much more to it than just the paper.

The purpose of this book is to help you put together your roadmap or legacy notebook — a guide for those who will represent you — your power of attorney, your mandatary or healthcare/financial proxy, and your executor.

I have divided the book into global sections — Attitudes & Feelings, People, Paper, Money, Digital Footprint, Stuff† and Legacy Items, and Final Wishes. Each section has a list of items to include — you customize each section to reflect your particular situation. Don't own a business? Ignore that part. Don't have investments? Nothing to list. Create your notebook to show who you are.

You will not find advice on what to put in your will or whom to name as your executor, nor will there be advice on how to invest or what to do with your items (though for that there are some suggestions). The

---

*Strictly speaking, the person named as your *power of attorney* is your **attorney**. I use the designation *power of attorney* so as not to confuse it with the word **attorney** defined as someone who practices law.

†**Stuff** — I have used the word *Stuff* as a nod to the late comedian George Carlin's riff on possessions. To see it on YouTube, search *George Carlin Stuff*

focus is on what you need to think about, and more importantly, put into written form for those who will represent you when you cannot do it yourself.

Your notebook format is the one you choose, though you might want to ask your designated power of attorney, mandatary/proxy, or executor (who may all be the same person) which format they would prefer. Mine, for example, will be paper AND saved to a USB flash drive (it is a work in progress). If you are going to design your own, you can use a loose-leaf binder, a bound notebook, an Excel spreadsheet, a Word document, or the pages at the back of this book. The possibilities are limited only by your requirements and imagination. If you decide to write it out by hand, do it in ink (except for passwords that change regularly) and make it legible. My handwriting is "chicken scratch" and I wouldn't ask anyone to try to interpret it, especially since they will be using it when I likely won't be able to speak for myself.

An additional enhancement, though not a definitive document, can be a video. In it, you can clarify your wishes as written in your legal documents. For your representatives, it will be much easier to find the information they need on paper or computer than having to scroll through a video, but additional clarity may well be appreciated (not to mention the emotional aspect of your near and dear being able to see and hear you once again). A video does not replace a legal paper will, power of attorney, or mandate in the event of incapacity. A video may confirm that you were of sound mind at the time you signed. Some even suggest making a video of the actual signing of the will.

The notebook you prepare will be (or should be) the most comprehensive collection of your personal data and should be kept securely. Paper copies, or password-protected USB flash drives used only when needed, are safer as long as they are kept in a secure place AND verified regularly. Data drives can fail, so while this is useful and will likely make life easier for your representatives, it would be good to create a hard copy. Paper may be copied but won't be hacked online.

If you use a password protected USB drive, make sure to give that password to at least one of your representatives. A backup copy is strongly recommended, preferably left outside of your home, perhaps with one of your trusted representatives. Be sure to verify your document from time to time and update when necessary. You may want to note the date of updates so you are certain of always having the latest version.

Initially, I contemplated having subscription-based online data storage but I decided against it for security reasons. Many of us bank online regularly with confidence, and some of us have a relatively large digital footprint, but I believe no online repository is hack-proof.

Because things change, it is a good idea to review your binder, notebook, or USB key once a year and revise where necessary. Think about how often you sign up for something online with a username and password. Most of us have a much bigger digital footprint than we realize, and all of those credentials need to be noted (including security challenge questions and answers) — and changed in our notebooks as needed. It may be useful to keep user IDs and passwords on a separate sheet that can be easily updated. When you update this document, make sure to destroy older versions to avoid future confusion.

Including your representatives in the document's preparation will give them a sense of what they will need to do in the future. They will also be better able to tell you which format works best for them. You need not divulge the contents of your will unless you want to, but you do need to let your representatives know where to find it when the time comes.

Each legacy notebook is unique. How you put yours together depends on what works best for you and for those who will step in to act on your behalf. This guide is a roadmap or checklist that will, I hope, make you think about what forms the bones of your life and what needs to be done for you when you can't do it yourself.

PART TWO

Attitudes & Feelings

Making changes
Retire
Leisure activities
New projects

Self-Worth
Don't be bullied
by family or by experts

A second opinion
may help

Relevance
Stay connected
Stay engaged

Changes in health
Keeping active

Changes in ability
Giving up the car keys
Accepting help

Activities
Hobbies
Volunteer work
Clubs

There are many milestones in our lives — the first words and steps, the first day of school, first love, education and graduation, career moves, maybe marriage, children, and grandchildren, losing a spouse to death or divorce, retirement, and inevitably, the final breath.

For many of us, it is not easy to talk about our last years. While we plan for marriage, children, jobs, vacations, and more, we do not always think of old age in the same way, other than perhaps saving some money to mitigate financial worries as we get older. Even people we perceive to be financially comfortable can struggle with the planning process.

Our worries about losing control of our finances, bodies, and minds extend to how we will live.

Changes can be useful, but some are difficult — think giving up the car keys, accepting help at home, or dealing with major health changes. Another big one is moving. Many people insist they will stay in their homes until the end — not the case for many.

Emotional issues extend to family as well. Often children are as resistant to talking about these matters as parents are to sharing their personal information. Siblings may disagree about the care of a parent who is ill or suffering from dementia — one may think home care is best, while the other insists on residential care. Arguments over money and goods once a parent is gone can be fraught with resentments and differences of opinion, not to mention the significant influence of sibling dynamics often stemming from childhood.

It is important to try to get everyone, more or less, on the same page. Corralling your adult children and making your wishes known can go a long way to resolving potential disputes between them after you are gone. In my experience and that of the experts I have consulted over the years, disagreements, or worse, bad blood and mistrust between siblings are among the major causes of discord in estate settlement.

Note that spousal intervention can also become an issue — spouses of beneficiary children, or spouses of the deceased who are not the parents of the children, may have opinions and desires that could create problems during estate settlement.

If you don't think your kids will be working in their mutual best interests without you around, make sure you consider that when you are choosing your representatives.

When you have that family discussion, you may want to consider involving an impartial third party to facilitate what can be a difficult conversation. A knowledgeable and compassionate outsider may provide a calming influence if conversations become contentious.

Life Changes

Moving from working to retirement can prompt questions about our relevance and how we stay connected and engaged in our communities. For many, this can be a wonderfully productive exercise and result in new friends, fulfilling projects, and new lines of work, both gainful and voluntary.

Another reality of this time of life is that not all of us can afford to stop working. If your only income sources are government benefits (Canada/ Québec Pension Plan, Old Age Security and the Guaranteed Income Supplement, or Social Security in the United States), your options are quite limited. Rent alone can eat up the lion's share of your monthly income, leaving precious little for necessities like food and medications, never mind a television or internet account, things which are essential to people who may not be able to do without because of disability, illness, or lack of mobility. Significant changes in circumstances can also have psychological effects.

Getting hired is more complicated, even for part-time jobs. We become less visible. Society is geared towards hiring younger people, and while it is nice to have someone offer a seat on the bus, we do get "deared" more often. As time marches on, professionals start to speak directly to our accompanying children, even when we are present in the room and perfectly capable of answering questions. This becomes more pronounced when we have visible disabilities, such as difficulty walking, speaking, hearing, or seeing.

There are many organizations and initiatives around to help us navigate our later lives — resource-sharing, from housing and cars to cooking and informal caregiving, as examples. However, it can be time-consuming to find them all. There doesn't seem to be a one-stop-shop that can help us put together all the necessary information and contacts, though some have tried to create one.

Overcoming the psychological hurdle of planning for old age is akin to buying an insurance policy. You put it in place, you update it from time to time, and you put it away until needed. Again, you can't plan for every eventuality. By putting in place some general guidelines, and critically, the information necessary for your representatives to take care of your affairs, you can provide some peace of mind for all concerned. Ensure those named know where to find your legacy notebook. There is no better gift to yourself, those who will care for you, and those you eventually leave behind than this roadmap (list).

Keep hold of your self-worth — stand up for yourself and don't allow yourself to be bullied by family, professionals, or well-intentioned acquaintances. What is right for your neighbour or your best friend may not be right for you. Know your limitations and work within them. Get a second opinion if you think it will be helpful. Don't be afraid to ask questions — the only stupid question is the one you don't ask when you are missing the answer. Do not hesitate to repeat questions when you need clarification.

Don't be embarrassed to ask for help. If you have been self-reliant all your life, asking for help seems like admitting that you are no longer competent. Get over it! Do for yourself what you can and be gracious about accepting help where you need it. When it comes to your money, try to ensure that the person you designate is someone you trust, or at the very least, someone with professional credentials and liability insurance. If you do choose an outside professional, be sure to check them out thoroughly before entrusting them with your funds and your personal information.

If you are the one who handles your family's financial life, educate your partner or children so that they know how to do it. If you are not the "managing" partner, this is something you need to learn.

Put together this plan, not just for your peace of mind, but for that of the people you will eventually leave behind. The work to prepare it may not be work you want to do, but once it is done, you will have established some control over what happens to you, your money, and your stuff. If you ever come to that place where your mind is no longer clear, at least you will have made known what you want. Again, ensure that your representatives know where to find it.

PART THREE

IF YOU LOVE THEM
LEAVE THEM
LISTS

Creating Your Roadmap
(Organizing Your Affairs)

People

YOU

Full Name
DOB
Birthplace
Social Insurance No
Social Security No (US)
Medicare card & location
Other nationality
information

CAREGIVERS

Caregiver 1
Caregiver 2

PERSONAL DELEGATES

Executor/Liquidator
Power of Attorney
Mandatary

EMERGENCY CONTACT

Primary
Alternate 1
Alternate 2

PROFESSIONAL ADVISORS

HEALTH
Doctors: GP & specialists
Pharmacy
Therapists

FINANCIAL
Financial advisor
Bank branch contact
Bank financial advisor

PROFESSIONAL
Lawyer
Notary
Accountant

EMPLOYER

Name
Position
Contact

CHILDREN & SIBLINGS

Name
Relationship
Name
Relationship

RELIGIOUS AFFILIATION

Contact
Place of worship

PETS

Pet name
Vet
Care person

This section should contain the contact information for all those individuals that play a part in your life — as well as yourself. Your representatives (power of attorney, mandatary or healthcare/financial proxy, executor/liquidator) need to know all kinds of things, so the first part of this section covers your personal information and contact coordinates for those who need to be informed when something has happened to you.

Personal information

You might think your family knows everything about you, but that isn't always the case. In this section you should start by listing all of your personal data:

- Full name and any additional names by which you may ever have been known
- Date and place of birth
- Social Insurance Number and location of card
- If you hold a United States Social Security Number, list it along with the card location
- If you have other nationalities, list them, along with the location of the supporting documents. If you don't have those documents, contact the closest embassy or consulate to find out how to get them. Assume they will be needed to settle your estate
- Driver's license, automobile registration, insurance information, and location of those documents
- Healthcare and hospital cards and where you keep them
- Written medical history — note major health events, current list of medications, allergies, immunizations, etc.

Your family

Your children may be the ones handling your affairs, or you may designate someone else. This is the place to list your siblings and your parents, if they are still living. It happens that sometimes there are half-siblings from other relationships, step-parents or siblings, and others close enough to qualify as family. Include them here as well. If your immediate family is not aware of some of the individuals from other relationships, this may help to put that information out into the open to avoid struggles for those you love once you are gone. Most important here is contact information so you will want to state their:

- Name(s)
- Address(es)
- Telephone numbers (mobile, landline, work line)
- Email address(es)
- Any other contact resources (Facebook Messenger, WhatsApp, Signal, for example).

Note that some of these items might be repeated in other sections. This booklet offers a guideline — when you make your notebook, you choose where you want this information to go or if you want to repeat it in other places.

Caregivers

If you are receiving in-home care, it is useful to list the name and contact information of the caregivers. If the care is being provided by an agency or a government organization, be sure to note the contact address, phone number and, if possible, a contact person's name, along with your file/dossier number with that organization.

Emergency contact

Your emergency contact(s) may be your children or siblings, a friend, a neighbour, or a trustee. The name and phone number are essential, and an email address is helpful as well.

If you are employed, either for pay or as a volunteer, you should list:

- Name of employer or volunteer organization
- Your position
- Contact name
- Contact phone
- Contact email

If you are self-employed or own one or more companies, you will need to create a separate section for that information, however you may want to include some contact information here.

If you are affiliated with a religion, have a spiritual advisor, or attend services at a particular place of worship, list the name and phone number of a contact there. This will be important for last rites or funeral considerations.

Personal delegates

This is perhaps the most important part of the People section besides family. The individuals you name here are the ones who will represent you, or in the event of incapacity, will become the legal *you*. Your representatives are the ones who will handle your personal affairs while you are still alive, including medical decisions if you are unable to make them yourself, and they will take care of what you leave behind, from clearing out your last residence to filing your final tax return.

If you live in Quebec, you make these arrangements through a notary or an attorney. In other places it will likely be an attorney. Note — a handwritten or holograph will, as it is called, is better than no will but will require more work for the executor. A holograph will is hand-written and unwitnessed. Your signature has to be identified and sworn to, and probate is generally required.

Your power of attorney (POA) represents you and, depending on the powers you grant in the POA document, can handle your financial affairs, real estate, medical decisions, and any other things that you allow. You generally need to put this in place while you are of sound mind — sooner rather than later. For example, you might want to introduce your power of attorney to your bank so that when they need to do something for you, the bank will already know who they are.

Note that these documents must be signed and registered while you are able to do so. If you develop dementia and are no longer considered competent to sign a legal document, you cannot make any more changes.

In Quebec, when you become incapacitated, your mandatary becomes you for legal purposes and takes over where the POA leaves off. There are equivalents across the country. Note that processing a mandate (or a similar document outside of Quebec) takes time, during which your representatives may run into some obstacles with financial institutions or other organizations. In other jurisdictions there may be a different designation, such as health-care proxy or financial proxy. Some places cover all of the roles with a single document; others require separate documents for each sphere of activity.

Your executor (liquidator in Quebec) is the person who will take over when you have passed on.

These roles can be assigned to one person, to several people, or to an institution such as a trust company. Note that financial advisors generally are not allowed to be legal representatives for their clients due to potential conflict of interest. Even if your jurisdiction allows it, you might be better served to choose someone else. Whichever way you decide to do it, this is the place to list the names and contact information.

Professional advisors

In this section you list the names and contact information for those people with whom you deal on specific matters.

Health

- Doctors & Dentists
- Pharmacy
- Therapists (occupational, psychological, massage, physio, recreational, etc.)

Financial

You may have just one or several — make sure to include them all.

- Financial Advisor
- Financial Planner
- Bank branch contact/Bank financial advisor
- Accountant and/or tax preparer
- Investment advisor/broker

Other professionals

▸ Lawyer
▸ Notary

Pets

If you share your life with an animal or three, you will need to list the contact information for the vet and for a care person — someone that you have designated to care for your pet(s) if you are incapable or have passed away. Listing their names and ages, as well as feeding information and special needs, is helpful as well.

Activity contacts

Keeping active is a big part of aging with grace. If you participate in various hobbies, sports teams or exercise regimens, clubs, volunteer work, or other activities (think gym memberships, dance classes, continuing education courses, volunteering at the local food bank or school…the list goes on), make sure to leave contact information of those who would need to be notified if you are unable to participate, or if you have died. This might be very important for the organizations that rely on you for volunteer work.

Note — I have found old address books quite helpful in finding the names of people to notify of a death. These days we most often keep them on our computers or phones, but our representatives should know where they are.

Paper

ESTATE & CARE DOCUMENTS

Will & any Codicils

Power of Attorney

Mandate (QC) or healthcare proxy (outside of QC)

Financial mandate or proxy, if separate document

DNR

HIPAA and/or POLST (US)

CIVIL DOCUMENTS

Birth certificate

Citizenship papers

Marriage certificate

Divorce documents

Death certificates for deceased spouse or child

Adoption agreements

PERSONAL DOCUMENTS

Driver's license/registration

Social Insurance Card

Social Security Card (US)

Any other nationality cards

Passport(s)

Nexus/Trusted Traveler cards

Medicare/Hospital cards

Medical insurance cards

CAA/AAA cards

Any other ID cards

LEGAL, FINANCIAL ARRANGEMENTS

Trust documents

Guardianship documents for minor children

INCOME SOURCE DOCUMENTS

Pension plan documents

Annuity documents/contact info

Provincial, State, Foreign pension contacts

FINANCIAL RECORDS

Investment documents & statements

Banking documents & statements

LOAN DOCUMENTS

Money you owe

Money owed you

BUSINESS DOCUMENTS

Business succession plan documents

We have much more paper in our lives than we know what to do with — and when we go, we leave it behind for someone else to handle. In this section, make sure to list the location of essential documents so they can be easily found. This may be a filing cabinet, a special accordion file, a binder — whatever you decide will work best for you. It might also be on one or more computer files, in which case you'll need to make any user IDs and passwords available. If you store any of this material in a safe, make sure your representatives have access to the key or the combination.

I live in Quebec and you will find in these pages frequent mentions of differences between procedures here and in other jurisdictions. Laws regarding succession here are slightly different from other places. For example, we rely on notaries to prepare our wills. A will registered with the Chambre des Notaires (Chamber of Notaries) does not need to be probated (probate is the legal process whereby a court confirms the validity of your will), though you will pay for a will search from both the Chambre and the Barreau du Québec (Quebec Bar Association). In other Canadian provinces, probate is generally required, though in some cases, probate can be replaced by a bond purchased through an insurance company. Make sure that you are aware of the procedures for your jurisdiction (see the Reference section for more details).

In the United States, laws can differ from state to state. Be sure to check out what is required in your state.

The most important documents for your representatives include:

- Your will and any codicils
- Your power of attorney (POA)
- Your mandate (Quebec) or healthcare proxy (other jurisdictions)
- Your financial mandate or proxy, if it is a separate document from the healthcare proxy, as is the case in Ontario and other jurisdictions.

- Your Do Not Resuscitate (DNR) document, if you have one. In the United States you may also have a POLST (Physician Orders for Life-Sustaining Treatment).
- In the United States you probably have a HIPAA document (Health Insurance Portability and Accountability Act of 1996), which specifies who can and cannot have access to your medical information.

Some people find it helpful to prepare a packet with copies of all necessary documents should there be an emergency where you cannot speak for yourself. This packet could include your DNR, healthcare proxy, power of attorney, POLST and HIPAA (in the United States), or any other related Lists. You might also want to include a sheet detailing your medical history.

Your representatives will also need to have access to your:

- Birth certificate
- Citizenship papers
- Marriage certificate
- Divorce documents
- Death certificates for a deceased spouse or child
- Adoption agreements

Note here that in some jurisdictions you might need different documents for each permission granted to a representative. The document you use for financial affairs may not be the same one as for medical affairs.

- Trust documents — These include living trusts, testamentary trusts, special situation trusts such as a Henson trust (or Quebec equivalent) for a disabled child or a Registered Disability Savings Plan (RDSP)
- Guardianship documents for minor children
- Pension plan documents and contact information
- Annuity documents and contact information
- Contact information for Service Canada, Retraite Québec
- Other provincial, state, or foreign pension organizations — these will all require your Social Insurance Number (Social Security number in the United States).

You will also need to specify the location of your:

- Driver's license
- Social Insurance card (Canada)
- Social Security card (if you are American)
- Any other nationality cards
- Passport(s)
- Nexus card or Trusted Traveler if you have one
- Medicare and hospital cards, medical insurance cards
- CAA or AAA cards if you belong to those organizations
- Any other identification cards

Your financial picture comes with lots of paper (or digital statements). You should provide the location of, or computer access information for:

- Investment documents and statements, especially the most recent
- Banking documents and statements
- Loan documents (money you owe, or money owed to you)

If you are a business owner and have papers that will be needed to transition the business upon your death, this is the place to list what those documents are and where they are located.

Again, having a designated place to keep your necessary documents can save an enormous amount of time for your representatives, and can help ensure that important assets or items are not overlooked. While your final tax returns need to be kept for seven years after your death, much of the other paper in your life can be disposed of after you no longer need it. Specify what needs to be conserved and your representatives can decide what to do with the rest.

Money - Assets

INCOME
Employment

PENSION PLAN
Employer pension plans
Private pension plans
Annuities
RRIFs

GOVERNMENT INCOME
Old Age Security
Canada Pension Plan or
Quebec Pension Plan
US Social Security

ONLINE BUSINESS INCOME
eBay
YouTube
PayPal
Amazon
Etsy

CONTACT INFORMATION FOR
Service Canada
Retraite Quebec
Provincial or foreign pension offices

BUSINESS INTERESTS
Name of business
Position:
Active owner/partner
Silent owner/partner

BANK ACCOUNTS
Bank name
Account number
Branch location
Branch phone number
Online banking login info

INVESTMENTS
Brokerage portfolio
Mutual funds portfolio
Investment property
Savings accounts

COLLECTIONS
Furniture
Art
Jewelry
Stamps/coins
Other

RETIREMENT PLANS
Registered Retirement Savings Plan (RRSP)
Tax-Free Savings Account (TFSA)
Individual Pension Plan (IPP)

FOR AMERICANS
IRA
Roth IRA
401K
Keogh plan

CARDS

LOYALTY CARDS
Optimum
Aeroplan
Air Miles
HBC
Chapters Indigo
Gas stations

GIFT & PREPAID CARDS

TRANSPORT CARDS
Opus card
Bus pass
Other travel passes

INSURANCE POLICIES
Critical Illness
Long-Term Care
Disability
Life
Home
Auto
Pet

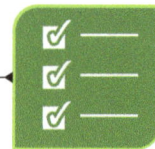

Whether you have a lot or a little, money greases the wheels of everyday life and we all have to deal with it, as do our representatives once we can't handle it anymore.

In this section, you should list anything that falls into your financial picture. This includes income, bank accounts, investments, insurance, business interests, bills that you need to pay (one-time and recurring), credit and loyalty cards, loans (from your mortgage(s) to the $500 you lent your brother-in-law last year), and finally the stuff with a resale value (collectible art, furniture, jewelry, special collections). In the Stuff section of this document, you can specify what should be done with those items having sentimental meaning but little or no monetary value.

Banks

Banks are often the centre of our financial lives. If you have a good relationship with your branch manager, he or she can be most helpful to your representative when the time comes. In this section, you should list all of your bank accounts, even if there isn't much money in them. Specify the branch, the account number, and the contact information including branch address. You may want to note login credentials as well, though those will be included in the Digital Legacy section. If you have a safety deposit box, make sure to note the box number and the location of the key. And if you find yourself with a plethora of bank accounts, you may consider consolidating a few of them.

Income

Income is another part of the money section. Your revenue may come from several sources — pensions, both government and private, RRIF income (Registered Retirement Income Fund), IRA or 401K if you are in the US, annuities held through insurance companies, business revenue, and so on. When listing these, you should specify where the money comes from, the contact information for the payors, and any account numbers for those revenue sources. If you are holding post-dated cheques for payment of a debt, your representative will need to contact the issuer to sort out what to do with them.

If you have a PayPal, eBay, Amazon, or Etsy account, you may derive income from those. Be sure to list all pertinent information for them, including account number, login credentials, and customer service contact information.

If you have foreign income (a foreign pension, for example, or income from foreign investments), you should make sure you list the source and any contact information necessary for your representative to make sure that account is closed (or transferred to a surviving spouse) upon your death.

Investments

Many of us have some kind of investments. Some may be financial, such as mutual fund accounts, brokerage accounts, GICs (Guaranteed Investment Certificates in Canada; CDs or certificates of deposit in the United States), and so on. Note that RRSPs (Registered Retirement Savings Plans), TFSAs (Tax-Free Savings Accounts), RRIFs (Registered Retirement Income Funds), and others are included under mutual fund or brokerage accounts, or investment accounts held at your bank. Investments in the United States may have similar umbrellas (Individual Retirement Account — IRA, 401K, Keogh plan, Roth IRA).

Investments can also include real estate, art, furniture, jewelry, stamps, coins, other collectibles, and so on. In this section, you should note any rental properties, second homes, such as a vacation cottage, or a time-share. All listings of these types of investments should include where they are located and estimated sale value, as well as any mortgages that might exist on those properties. For a time-share property or a condo, include the contact information for the property management office.

Insurance

Part of your financial picture probably includes some insurance policies. You might have life insurance, health insurance, a group plan, mortgage insurance with your mortgage lender or held privately, travel insurance, long-term care and/or critical illness coverage, annuities (mentioned above), and segregated funds (as part of mutual fund investments). Here you need to include policy numbers, issuer information, and the name of the insurance broker, if you have one. You may also note the face value of the life policies.

Note that in the United States, where healthcare is, for the most part, private, medical insurance plans are essential. If you have coverage there or live in the United States, make note of those plans as well.

Businesses and other assets

If you have business interests, you can deal with them either in a separate section or just note the necessary information in the Money section. At the very least, you should list the name of the business, your role in it, and the contact information of anyone who would need to be notified of your situation. As a business owner you will most likely have made succession plans (if you haven't, you need to).

A sometimes-overlooked asset can be loyalty cards — anything from your pharmacy and grocery stores to air miles or other cards that accumulate points. List the account numbers and the providers, the location of the cards, and if you have it, a phone number. Air mileage points and loyalty points may be transferable — check with the provider and note that in your legacy notebook.

Speaking of loyalty cards, don't forget about memberships like Costco, CAA, AAA, FADOQ, CARP, AARP, and countless others. Check to see what cards are in your wallet, on your keyring, or in your purse (or that drawer in which you drop things you don't use too often).

Money - Debts

DEBTS

Mortgages
Credit cards
Personal loans
Business loans
Lines of credit
Payment plans

AUTOMATED TRANSACTIONS

Bill payments
Subscriptions
Charitable donations
Savings transfers

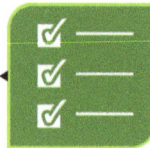

CARDS

MAJOR CREDIT CARDS

American Express
VISA
MasterCard
Discover

OTHER CREDIT CARDS

PC Financial
Triangle
Walmart
Home Depot
Department store

OTHER BILLS

QUARTERLY INCOME TAX INSTALLMENTS

Revenu Quebec
Canada Revenue Agency

UTILITIES

Electricity
Gas
Oil
Water bill

HOUSING COSTS

Rent
Mortgage
Condo fees
Property taxes
School taxes

COMMUNICATION & ENTERTAINMENT

Internet service
Cell phone
Land line
Television
Streaming services, Netflix, Crave, etc.

SERVICES

Cleaning service
Landscaper/snow removal

Debts need to be taken care of as well. Here is the place to list loans, both those you owe and those owed to you. This includes mortgages (see above on second properties), car loans, consumer proposals, layaway plans, loans from appliance and furniture stores, and any other debts that you are paying off. Where money is owed to you, list the debtor's name and contact information, as well as the amount owing.

Credit cards may be listed as part of the banking accounts or separately. Make sure to list the card numbers and any long-term outstanding amounts as well as contact information. In addition to the usual Visa and MasterCard, you may have cards tied to specific entities (The Bay, The Brick, etc.). Make sure you also note any cards held in other countries — for example, a Canadian might have a card for a United States department store (Macy's, Bloomingdale's).

If you have a line of credit, it may be dealt with easily at the bank, though some details should be checked. You may have credit insurance that will pay off the credit line balance in the event of your death (and sometimes in case of disability). Make sure to include the account in your list of bank accounts, and if it is insured, make a note of that as well. Other debt accounts may also be insured. Typically, financial institutions offer insurance on mortgages, credit cards, and lines of credit.

You may have some or all of the financial items discussed here, and that should be enough to provoke thoughts about what you have and need to include. Each of us has a unique list.

Digital Footprint

COMPUTERS

Destruction of personal files

Files to be passed on

CLOUD STORAGE

One Drive
iCloud
Online backup services
Dropbox

EMAIL ADDRESSES

User ID
Password

WEBSITES

Domain name
Administrator

ONLINE SUBSCRIPTIONS

NEWS & EZINES

NEWSPAPERS
Gazette
Le Devoir
Globe & Mail
NY Times
Washington Post

MAGAZINES
New Yorker
Maclean's
Chatelaine
Wired

SOCIAL
Facebook
Myspace
Google
Instagram
Twitter
Snapchat
YouTube
Vimeo

PROFESSIONAL
LinkedIn
Work-related sites

GAMING
Game name
Website
User login

ACCOUNTS • BUY/SELL
eBay
Amazon
Etsy

You may not think you have much of a digital footprint, but you could be surprised when you sit down to list all of your usernames and passwords. After you complete this, you might think twice about how many things you sign on to — I know I have.

While much of the information in this roadmap won't often change, if at all, you might want to keep your passwords on a separate page that can be updated easily. You may also consider using a password management program such as LastPass or Dashlane (Apple products have Keychain built-in). There are a number of them available, some free, some entailing a fee. The password manager's advantage is that you will only need to leave your representative the user ID and master password for that application — all the other passwords and websites will be found inside that manager. If you choose to create your notebook in a loose-leaf binder, look for one that has an attached pocket inside. It's a handy place to keep the password list, the safety deposit box key, and anything else that is easy to misplace. You can also purchase loose-leaf style pocket inserts that do the same thing. Another way to keep passwords is to use a small address book and write them in under the appropriate letter.

It is important to list both usernames/IDs and passwords. Listing your security questions and answers could be helpful when your representative has difficulty logging in. Passwords are useless without a user ID. While user IDs are frequently email addresses, this isn't always the case.

Important to note — keep this password list in a safe place. If you have it on a USB key, you may want to password-protect the key, but be sure to tell your representatives not only where the key is, but what the password is.

Here is a sample list, which is by no means exhaustive — yours may be substantially different.

- Bank accounts
- Investment accounts
- PayPal, Etsy, eBay, Amazon, and other revenue-producing accounts
- Professional websites (ones that you use for work)
- Email accounts
- Yahoo mail
- Gmail
- Outlook and web-based Outlook mail or Hotmail
- Microsoft Exchange
- Other accounts linked to your personal websites or work logins
- Credentials to log on to your devices — computers, tablets, mobile phones, and so on

Subscriptions

Many of our subscriptions are digital these days, so this topic is included in your digital legacy. However, there are still many who receive paper subscriptions to newspapers and magazines. Subscription information, with a note indicating that it is paper based, can be included in this section.

- Newspapers — The Globe & Mail, Montreal Gazette, The New York Times, The Washington Post, The Guardian
- Online magazines — The New Yorker, Vogue, Slate, Wired, Costco
- Gaming sites (all kinds of games, even things like The New York Times Crossword)

Note that payments for some of these sites may be, whether you have done it deliberately or not, set to auto-renew yearly or monthly. Make sure you note which auto-renew, so those payments can be cancelled.

Social media

A sample (but not exhaustive) list — you know which ones you are on.

- Facebook
- Instagram
- Snapchat
- Vimeo
- YouTube
- Tik-Tok
- Twitter
- Professional social media counts too – e.g. LinkedIn

If you participate in forums like Reddit, Quora, or those linked to HP or Apple vendors, you will probably have login credentials there too.

If you have an online dating profile, make sure to include those credentials as well, otherwise you may be looking for love long after you have gone to the great beyond.

Email & web domains

You may have one or many email accounts. For your representative to notify those who communicate with you regularly, or to be able to cancel the account, you will need to provide your login information. These can go on your separate password sheet, or they might be included in your password manager.

If you own one or more web domains, you need to make arrangements for what will happen to them. Sometimes this will come in the context of business succession planning, but if you aren't in that situation, you could still have things online. Do you write a blog or produce videos for YouTube or Vimeo? Do you have a small business that you share with a partner? Who is the host of your website or blog?

And then there is cloud storage — if you use online backup and storage accounts (CrashPlan, iCloud, One Drive, Dropbox), your representative will need to close them and destroy the data unless you specify otherwise.

Note that some social media sites will not allow posthumous modification without proper paperwork, or sometimes even with proper paperwork, and will likely require user ID and password. Facebook, for example, will allow the estate to memorialize but not delete an account. If you have the user ID and password, you can do whatever you like. Don't let embarrassment keep you from making the list complete. You may not want your family to know what your Internet activities include, but if those sites send you email, they will likely find out anyway. At least this way they can shut down the subscriptions. These sites might include online dating or adult videos.

Digital photos are another important part of our lives now. We store them on our computers, tablets, and phones. Often, we keep copies online (iCloud Photos, Amazon, Flickr, and others). You may consider printing those you want to save for posterity. Make sure your representatives know how to access them and what you want to be done with them.

In the end, if you miss one or two sites, eventually the service will likely delete you for non-use, but it is best if your representative can close down as many as possible.

Hardware is the other part of your digital legacy. If you have computers and external hard drives (including flash drives), there should be arrangements for the destruction of data that isn't designated to be passed on, as well as for disposal of equipment. Hardware should be thoroughly and professionally cleaned, digitally and physically, if it is going to be sold. If you are leaving these things to family, it becomes a matter of choice.

Your mobile phone needs to be dealt with as well. A smartphone should be treated as a tablet for cleaning and preservation purposes. It may be worthwhile to have that done professionally to ensure thorough clearing of all personal information. Note that the contacts on a phone may be very useful for your representative, so they may want to delay that cleaning until everything else is done.

This section of your notebook may be the most time-consuming to prepare, depending on how digitally active you are. It is also the section that is most likely to change often and which, for obvious reasons, needs the most protection.

Stuff and Legacy Items

EMOTIONAL VS REAL VALUE

Real market value

Emotional attachment value

WHAT DO THE KIDS WANT TO HAVE

We live longer. Our kids have their own stuff and don't want most of ours.

HANDLING COLLECTIBLES

Confirm values
Select disposal options
Auction
Private sale

GIFTING TO FAMILY
Gifts should be unconditional. Don't specify how they should be dealt with once in the hands of the recipient.

GIFTING TO CHARITY
Give directly
Sell and give proceeds to charity

PERSONAL GOODS
NO MONETARY VALUE

Household goods
Non-collectible furniture
Clothing
Books
Photographs
Household decor

WHAT TO DO WITH THE REST

REPURPOSING

DONATE TO
VARIOUS ORGANIZATIONS
Renaissance
Salvation Army
Mada
ReStore
Le Chainon
QC Association for the Disabled
Freecycle.org

DISPOSE OF
Ecocentre
Curbside collection

No matter how much or how little we have, when we are gone, there is stuff to take care of: furniture, kitchenware, household goods, clothing, decorative items, photo albums, books, electronics (digital equipment such as computers and phones are dealt with in the Digital Footprint section), and much more.

As you work through this section, it is important to distinguish between monetary (market) value and emotional value. Some items have tremendous value to us personally but no market value. Your list should focus on those items with a monetary value. If you have written evaluations, reference them in your notebook so your representative can find them. If you have things that need to be sold by auction, and you have a preference as to which auction house to use, provide the contact information.

For other household items and furnishings, you may want to designate to whom you wish them to go or note if they are to be sold or donated. If you have specific bequests to family members, friends, or charities, list those items and the contact information for the recipients.

Over time, I have learned that stuff can be more of a burden than a blessing. Many of us live longer than previous generations, and our kids generally don't want our stuff. They have already furnished their nests. In our 60s and 70s we have lived the longer parts of our lives and often still have living parents. When I was closing out my mother's place, the local fire inspector told me that he and his wife live with not only the pieces they acquired themselves early on, but with what they had inherited from her parents and her parents' parents — their kids don't want any of it.

Sorting through clothing can be a daunting task. If your house is being cleared out because you have moved, you will still need some of your clothes, but there is often much that needs to be disposed of. Vintage dealers may take some of the retro trendy clothing, but consignment shops are often picky about style and quality, so much will end up being donated or tossed. If you can

One of my clients ended up buying back family items from the estate auction because no provision had been made in the will for family members to retain desired pieces.

My grandfather was a prolific painter. He left behind a treasure trove of paintings that chronicled his life. He died in the mid-1970s, leaving his only child, my father, to deal with his works. Only... my father didn't. Two years before his death in 2009, my father announced that I should "do something with the paintings". I dutifully photographed them and started to look into how to get them exhibited. Then life intervened and I did not have time to pursue it. Time went on. My mother was moved to a residence and the house was sold. I am still sitting with this legacy, and a portion of my retirement years will be spent on this project. Ideally, my father would have dealt with this — I don't know why he didn't. I resent that he pushed it off on me. And yet... I adored my grandfather and was around when he painted many of them. It will be an opportunity to pay homage to him, to ensure his work becomes known. I don't want to leave it to my kids.

reduce the closet contents in advance, great. If not, at least note here what you want to be done with your clothes. Many organizations accept clothing donations.

If you have hobbies — train sets, needlecrafts, pottery, photography, model building, woodworking, fishing — the list is endless — be sure to make notes about their disposition.

You can help your representatives by listing contacts, if you have any, for selling your things.

Some other thoughts – legacy items

Some items either have a long family legacy or may have been handed to you with the responsibility to "do something" with them. You may feel an obligation to deliver on promises made to parents or others who have put you in this position. Decisions around items like this are fraught with emotion, guilt, and sometimes, resentment.

If the items in question have no personal value to you or other family members or friends (and you have asked them all), then you need to decide how best to dispose of them. If they have monetary value, you may want to instruct your representatives to sell them. If their value is strictly an emotional attachment, then you can dispose of them in whatever way is easiest for you. On the other hand, if you are interested in making a project out of it, you might take a fascinating journey into family history. You may be doing this for your parents or older relatives. Your representatives will be doing it for you, so let them know how you want your stuff handled.

A bit of a recap:

Ask your kids (and other family members and friends, if that is warranted) what they want to have and mark those items — or give them away immediately (unless, of course, you are still using them).

Assess your stuff to determine what has real value versus sentimental value. If you have collectibles, have a professional evaluation done, if you haven't already, and decide how you want to dispose of them, or instruct your executor to do it. Options for disposition include auctions, private sales, gifting to family, friends, or charity. Refugee organizations are frequently on the lookout for usable furniture and clothing to help those newly arrived. Items left at the end of your driveway (or on the street if you are in an apartment) also often find their way to new homes. The Freecycle Network (freecycle.org), which has online listings across the United States, Canada, and many other countries, is a great way to rehome items that still have life in them. As the old saying goes, one person's trash is another's treasure.

For everything else there are three essential choices — repurposing, donating, or disposal. Not everything will need your input but mention those things that are important to you. You need only go into as much detail as you feel necessary. What you don't specify will be dealt with, though it may be in a way different from what you might have done.

You are not obliged to reveal the contents of your will to anyone, and to whom you leave personal items is up to you as well. You may want to give away some items before you pass away (with a warm hand, as my mother liked to say), but remember that once you have given it away, whether it is an object or money, you no longer have a say in how it is to be used. You may exert some control from beyond the grave with family trusts however, and that is a discussion to have with your financial and legal advisors.

Final Wishes

PERSONAL WISHES

☑ ——
☑ ——
☑ ——

TYPE OF BURIAL OR CREMATION

☑ ——
☑ ——
☑ ——

PRE-ARRANGEMENTS

☑ ——
☑ ——
☑ ——

FUNERAL HOME

☑ ——
☑ ——
☑ ——

TO BE NOTIFIED AT DEATH

Relatives
Friends
Business contacts
Volunteer contacts
Religious contacts

REGULAR CONTACTS

Bank
Investment advisor

UTILITIES

Gas
Electricity
Television
Internet
Telephone
   - Land line
   - Cell phone

PENSION PLANS

GOVERNMENT

Service Canada
   - Social insurance
   - Old Age Security
QPP/CPP
US Social Security

☑ ——
☑ ——
☑ ——

Now we come to the part we don't really want to think about too much — when the instructions in this section are followed, it means we are no longer here.

What do you want to happen to your body? Burial, cremation, becoming a tree? Is there a funeral home that your family uses? Have you made pre-arrangements? Are there particular rituals in which you would like to have a say? You may also want to have a discussion with your spiritual advisor before you complete this section.

If you want to be buried or cremated, the arrangements can be relatively straightforward. Very few jurisdictions are on board with you being planted and feeding a tree, though the options are increasing. If you have made arrangements, and more importantly, if you have already paid for them, you need to make sure your representatives know what those arrangements are — note them here. If you intend to donate your body to science, write down the details of what you have planned.

If you have specific wishes for how your memorial should be conducted, this is the place to list them as well. Want a bagpiper to play Amazing Grace? Write it down. Not interested in a funeral? Be clear about it. How about a memorial celebration? Do you want it at home? At your favourite restaurant? At the funeral home? Don't leave it to chance — write it down here. Our final wishes are as individual as we are, but unless we let our representatives know, the final rituals, or lack thereof, will be at the discretion of someone else.

Thinking about incapacity and death isn't a cheerful activity. We tend to avoid it as much as possible, even though most of us know that we should give it a bit of time every so often. Some of us approach it with careful consideration; others go for the "What do I care — I'll be dead" option. Consider carefully what is truly important to you, what values you would want to be expressed in your final instructions.

The reality doesn't go away, even if we don't deal with it, and that niggling discomfort lingers in the background. Writing a will does not mean you will die tomorrow. Buying insurance will not hasten your demise. You buy car and home insurance easily, and it gives you peace of mind. You don't buy it with the thought that you will have an accident or a house catastrophe next week. These things are part of the foundation of our financial lives. Final years planning need not be different — put it in place, review from time to time (as you should do with your will, POA and mandate/proxy documents, not to mention life insurance), and give yourself, and your near and dear, the peace of mind that can come from having put these instructions in place.

Writing this in the midst of the 2020-21 COVID-19 pandemic, I have become keenly aware that the preparation of a legacy note-book has taken on an even more pressing relevance. In uncertain times like these, where your representatives may be equally at risk, written instructions become that much more critical.

PART FOUR

The Lists

A Word About the Lists

A guide such as this would not be complete without lists to help you design your own book. The beginning of each section of this guide has a corresponding colour-coordinated *map* with a list of examples. The lists for each section are colour coordinated with the maps, helping you to keep your entries organized and ensuring that you don't miss sections.

While many of the listed items likely apply to most of us, you could have some items to record that we have not discussed, or even considered. Your entries may be quite different from the ones suggested in the text. While this is true for all sections, it may be particularly apt for the Digital Footprint section — there are so many websites that could be included, and your list will reflect your interests and activities.

These Lists may be used as a starting place for your own design, or as described, using the *Other* pages to add information for which the lists in this book have not provided enough space.

The incapacity or death of a loved one is hard enough for those left behind. The notebook, in whatever form you choose, may be the most useful part of the legacy you leave for your family and your representatives. The bonus for you? Getting this done will give you peace of mind, secure in the knowledge that you have done all you can to make management of the last part of your life easier.

YOU
This is your personal information and yours alone

Full Name _____

Also known as names _____

Date of birth _____

Birthplace _____

Social Insurance N° _____

Social Security N° (US) _____

Other nationality information 1 _____

Other nationality information 2 _____

FAMILY & FRIENDS
List spouse, parents, children, siblings, close friends

Emergency contact 1 _____Relationship _____

Address _____

Tel C _____H_____W_____

E-mail 1 _____ 2 _____

Emergency contact 2 _____Relationship _____

Address _____

Tel C _____H_____W_____

E-mail 1 _____ 2 _____

Name _____Relationship _____

Address _____

Tel C _____H_____W_____

E-mail 1 _____ 2 _____

Notes _____

_____

FAMILY & FRIENDS *List spouse, parents, children, siblings, close friends*

Name _____ Relationship _____

Address _____

Tel C _____ H _____ W _____

E-mail 1 _____ 2 _____

Name _____ Relationship _____

Address _____

Tel C _____ H _____ W _____

E-mail 1 _____ 2 _____

Name _____ Relationship _____

Address _____

Tel C _____ H _____ W _____

E-mail 1 _____ 2 _____

Name _____ Relationship _____

Address _____

Tel C _____ H _____ W _____

E-mail 1 _____ 2 _____

Name _____ Relationship _____

Address _____

Tel C _____ H _____ W _____

E-mail 1 _____ 2 _____

Notes _____

_____

_____

FAMILY & FRIENDS *List spouse, parents, children, siblings, close friends*

Name _____Relationship _____

Address _____

Tel C_____H_____W_____

E-mail 1 _____ 2 _____

Name _____Relationship _____

Address _____

Tel C_____H_____W_____

E-mail 1 _____ 2 _____

Name _____Relationship _____

Address _____

Tel C_____H_____W_____

E-mail 1 _____ 2 _____

Name _____Relationship _____

Address _____

Tel C_____H_____W_____

E-mail 1 _____ 2 _____

Name _____Relationship _____

Address _____

Tel C_____H_____W_____

E-mail 1 _____ 2 _____

Notes_____

_____

_____

CAREGIVERS
People who provide for your care

Company Name _____

Tel _____ E-mail _____

Caregiver Name _____

Tel _____ E-mail _____

Company Name _____

Tel _____ E-mail _____

Caregiver Name _____

Tel _____ E-mail _____

PERSONAL DELEGATES
People in charge of your affairs

Executor/Liquidator _____

Address _____

Tel C_____ H_____ W_____

E-mail 1 _____ 2 _____

Other contact info _____

Power of Attorney _____

Address _____

Tel C_____ H_____ W_____

E-mail 1 _____ 2 _____

Other contact info _____

Notes _____

_____

_____

_____

PERSONAL DELEGATES *People in charge of your affairs*

Mandatary (Healthcare/Financial Proxy QC) _____

Address _____

Tel C_____ H_____ W_____

E-mail 1 _____ 2 _____

Other contact info _____

Healthcare and/or Financial Proxy_____

Address _____

Tel C_____ H_____ W____

E-mail 1 _____ 2 _____

Other contact info _____

HEALTH PROFESSIONAL ADVISORS
List your doctors, therapists, dentist, pharmacist

Provider _____

Profession/Name _____

Tel W _____ext_____C_____

E-mail 1 _____ 2 _____

Address _____

Provider _____

Profession/Name _____

Tel W _____ext_____C_____

E-mail 1 _____ 2 _____

Address _____

Notes_____

_____

HEALTH PROFESSIONAL ADVISORS *doctors, therapists, dentist, pharmacist*

Provider _____

Profession/Name _____

Tel W _____ ext_____ C_____

E-mail 1 _____ 2 _____

Address _____

Provider _____

Profession/Name _____

Tel W _____ ext_____ C_____

E-mail 1 _____ 2 _____

Address _____

Provider _____

Profession/Name _____

Tel W _____ ext_____ C_____

E-mail 1 _____ 2 _____

Address _____

Provider _____

Profession/Name _____

Tel W _____ ext_____ C_____

E-mail 1 _____ 2 _____

Address _____

Notes_____

_____

_____

_____

HEALTH PROFESSIONAL ADVISORS *doctors, therapists, dentist, pharmacist*

Provider _____

Profession/Name _____

Tel W _____ext_____C_____

E-mail 1 _____ 2 _____

Address _____

FINANCIAL PROFESSIONAL ADVISORS
List your bank contact, accountant/tax preparer, financial advisor

Provider _____

Profession/Name _____

Tel W _____ext_____C_____

E-mail 1 _____ 2 _____

Address _____

Provider _____

Profession/Name _____

Tel W _____ext_____C_____

E-mail 1 _____ 2 _____

Address _____

Provider _____

Profession/Name _____

Tel W _____ext_____C_____

E-mail 1 _____ 2 _____

Address _____

Notes_____

_____

LEGAL PROFESSIONAL ADVISORS
List your lawyer, notary, and other legal professionals

Provider _____

Profession/Name _____

Tel W _____ ext_____ C_____

E-mail 1 _____ 2 _____

Address _____

Provider _____

Profession/Name _____

Tel W _____ ext_____ C_____

E-mail 1 _____ 2 _____

Address _____

Provider _____

Profession/Name _____

Tel W _____ ext_____ C_____

E-mail 1 _____ 2 _____

Address _____

Provider _____

Profession/Name _____

Tel W _____ ext_____ C_____

E-mail 1 _____ 2 _____

Address _____

Notes _____

_____

_____

EMPLOYER
This is your boss or human resources contact

Company name _____

Contact name _____

Tel W _____ ext_____ C_____

E-mail 1 _____ 2 _____

My position_____

RELIGIOUS/SPIRITUAL AFFILIATION
List place of worship and spiritual advisor

Name_____Relationship _____

Address _____

Tel W _____ ext_____ C_____

E-mail 1 _____ 2 _____

CHARITY/VOLUNTEER AFFILIATIONS
List organizations and contacts

Name_____Relationship _____

Address _____

Tel W _____ ext_____ C_____

E-mail 1 _____ 2 _____

Name_____Relationship _____

Address _____

Tel W _____ ext_____ C_____

E-mail 1 _____ 2 _____

Notes_____

_____

_____

CLUBS
Example: Sporting, quilting, book, birding, your leisure and fun activities

Club _____Type _____

Contact _____

Tel W _____ext_____C_____

E-mail 1 _____ 2 _____

Club _____Type _____

Contact _____

Tel W _____ext_____C_____

E-mail 1 _____ 2 _____

Club _____Type _____

Contact _____

Tel W _____ext_____C_____

E-mail 1 _____ 2 _____

PETS
Your friends and companions

Name _____

Type/Breed _____

Date of birth/Age _____

Veterinarian name _____

Vet Tel W _____ext_____C_____

Care person _____

Tel C_____H_____W_____

Care and feeding notes _____

_____

Medical information_____

PETS *your friends and companions*

Name _____

Type/Breed _____

Date of birth/Age _____

Veterinarian name _____

Vet Tel W _____ ext _____ C _____

Care person _____

Tel C _____ H _____ W _____

Care and feeding notes _____

_____

Medical information _____

Name _____

Type/Breed _____

Date of birth/Age _____

Veterinarian name _____

Vet Tel W _____ ext _____ C _____

Care person _____

Tel C _____ H _____ W _____

Care and feeding notes _____

_____

Medical information _____

Notes _____

_____

_____

_____

_____

_____

THIS SECTION LAST UPDATED: _____

ESTATE & CARE DOCUMENTS
*List the **locations** of your important care & estate documents*

Power of Attorney _____

Mandate (QC)_____

Healthcare proxy (outside of QC) _____

Will and **codicils** _____

DNR _____

HIPAA and/or **POLST** (US)_____

Other_____

CIVIL DOCUMENTS
List the locations of your birth, marriage, divorce and death certificates

Birth certificate _____

Citizenship papers _____

Marriage certificate _____

Divorce documents_____

Death certificates (deceased spouse or child) _____

Adoption agreements _____

Other_____

PERSONAL DOCUMENTS
List the locations of your important cards and passport(s)

Driver's license/registration _____Nº _____

Social Insurance Card _____Nº _____

Social Security Card (US) _____Nº _____

Any **other nationality** cards _____Nº _____

Passport(s) _____Nº _____

Nexus/Trusted Traveler cards_____Nº _____

_____

DNR - Do Not Resuscitate | **POLST** - Physician Orders for Life-Sustaining Treatment
HIPAA - Health Insurance Portability and Accountability Act

PERSONAL DOCUMENTS *locations of your important cards*

Medicare/Hospital cards _____ Nº _____

Medical insurance cards _____ Nº _____

Other_____

LEGAL/FINANCIAL ARRANGEMENTS
List the locations of your trust documents & guardianship documents for minors

Trust documents _____

Guardianship documents for minor children _____

Other_____

INCOME SOURCE
List the locations of your income agreements & documents

Pension plan documents _____

Annuity documents/contact info _____

Provincial, State, Foreign pension contacts_____

Other_____

FINANCIAL RECORDS
List the locations of your financial statements and records

Investment documents & statements _____

Banking documents & statements _____

Loan: money you owe _____

Loan: money owed you _____

BUSINESS DOCUMENTS
List the location of your plans for the future of your business

Business succession plan_____

Other_____

_____

BANKS
List your banks, bank branches and credit unions

Name _____ Branch Nº _____

Acct Nº _____ Type _____

Contact 1 _____ 2 _____

Tel W _____ ext _____

Name _____ Branch Nº _____

Acct Nº _____ Type _____

Contact 1 _____ 2 _____

Tel W _____ ext _____

Name _____ Branch Nº _____

Acct Nº _____ Type _____

Contact 1 _____ 2 _____

Tel W _____ ext _____

Name _____ Branch Nº _____

Acct Nº _____ Type _____

Contact 1 _____ 2 _____

Tel W _____ ext _____

INCOME
List your working income

Source 1 _____ Salary _____

Contact _____ Tel _____

Auto deposit to _____ Acct Nº _____

Notes _____

_____

INCOME   *List your working income*

Source 2 _____   Salary _____

Contact _____   Tel _____

Auto deposit to _____   Acct Nº _____

ONLINE BUSINESS INCOME
Example: YouTube, eBay, Amazon, Etsy, PayPal and other online income accounts

Company 1 _____   Acct Nº _____

Contact info _____

Company 2 _____   Acct Nº _____

Contact info _____

Company 3 _____   Acct Nº _____

Contact info _____

Company 4 _____   Acct Nº _____

Contact info _____

PENSIONS
List your company pensions

Payor _____   Acct Nº _____

Contact _____   Tel _____

Auto deposit to _____   Acct Nº _____

Payor _____   Acct Nº _____

Contact _____   Tel _____

Auto deposit to _____   Acct Nº _____

PENSIONS *List your company pensions*

Payor _____ Acct Nº _____

Contact _____ Tel _____

Auto deposit to _____ Acct Nº _____

GOVERNMENT
List your prov/state or federal pensions

Prov/State _____ Acct Nº _____

Contact _____ Tel _____

Auto deposit to _____ Acct Nº _____

Federal _____ Acct Nº _____

Contact _____ Tel _____

Auto deposit to _____ Acct Nº _____

Foreign (Country) _____ Acct Nº _____

Contact _____ Tel _____

Auto deposit to _____ Acct Nº _____

ANNUITIES
List your annuity sources

Payor _____ Acct Nº _____

Contact _____ Tel _____

Auto deposit to _____ Acct Nº _____

Payor _____ Acct Nº _____

Contact _____ Tel _____

Auto deposit to _____ Acct Nº _____

RETIREMENT PLAN INCOME
List your retirement income funds: RRIF, LRIF, LIF, IRA, 401K, Keogh, other

PLAN _____ Acct Nº _____

Payor _____ Tel _____

Auto deposit to _____ Acct Nº _____

PLAN _____ Acct Nº _____

Payor _____ Tel _____

Auto deposit to _____ Acct Nº _____

PLAN _____ Acct Nº _____

Payor _____ Tel _____

Auto deposit to _____ Acct Nº _____

PLAN _____ Acct Nº _____

Payor _____ Tel _____

Auto deposit to _____ Acct Nº _____

AUTOMOBILES AND OTHER VEHICLES
List your cars, trucks, recreational vehicles (including RVs) and others

Vehicle 1 _____ License plate _____

Loan/Lease _____ Tel _____

Vehicle 2 _____ License plate _____

Loan/Lease _____ Tel _____

Vehicle 3 _____ License plate _____

Loan/Lease _____ Tel _____

Vehicle 4 _____ License plate _____

Loan/Lease _____ Tel _____

INVESTMENTS AND HOLDINGS
List your different investment properties and possessions

Real Estate Primary residence _____

Address _____

Prop. Mgr. (if applicable)_____ Contact_____

Tel W _____ext_____ C_____

Location of deeds and other documents_____

Mortgage lender _____ Contact_____

Tel W _____ext_____ C_____

Condo fees _____ Property mgr._____

Tel W_____ext_____ C_____

Acct. Nº _____ Contact_____Tel_____

Property tax 1 _____ Co. _____

Acct. Nº _____ Contact_____Tel_____

School tax 1_____ Co. _____

Acct. Nº _____ Contact_____Tel_____

Real Estate Secondary property _____

Address _____

Prop. Mgr. (if applicable)_____ Contact_____

Tel W_____ext_____ C_____

Location of deeds and other documents_____

Mortgage lender _____ Contact_____

Tel W _____ext_____ C_____

Condo fees _____ Property mgr. _____

Acct. Nº _____ Contact_____Tel _____

Property tax 2 _____ Co._____

Acct. Nº _____ Contact_____Tel _____

INVESTMENTS AND HOLDINGS *List your different investment properties and possessions*

School tax 2_____Co. _____

Acct. Nº _____ Contact_____Tel _____

Real Estate Investment property _____

Address _____

Prop. Mgr. (if applicable)_____Contact_____

Tel W_____ext_____C_____

Location of deeds and other documents_____

Mortgage lender _____Contact_____

Tel W _____ext_____C_____

Condo fees _____Property mgr._____

Acct. Nº _____ Contact_____Tel _____

Property tax 3 _____Co. _____

Acct. Nº _____ Contact_____Tel _____

School tax 3_____Co. _____

Acct. Nº _____ Contact_____Tel _____

INVESTMENT ACCOUNTS
List your non-registered investment plans

Brokerage house _____

Contact_____Acct Nº _____

Tel W _____ext_____C_____

E-mail 1 _____ 2 _____

Brokerage house _____

Contact_____Acct Nº _____

Tel W _____ext_____C_____

E-mail 1 _____ 2 _____

INVESTMENTS - OTHER
List your different investment possessions

Furniture_____

Inventory list location _____

Evaluations list _____

Provenance documents _____

Location _____

Disposition contact _____

Tel W _____ext_____C_____

Art_____

Inventory list location _____

Evaluations list _____

Provenance documents _____

Disposition contact _____

Tel W _____ext_____C_____

Stamps/coins _____

Evaluations list _____

Provenance documents _____

Location _____

Disposition contact _____

Tel W _____ext_____C_____

Notes_____

_____

_____

_____

_____

_____

INVESTMENTS - OTHER   *List your different investment possessions*

Jewelry _____

Inventory list location _____

Evaluations list _____

Provenance documents _____

Location _____

Disposition contact _____

Tel W _____ ext _____ C_____

Other _____

Description _____

Evaluations list _____

Provenance documents _____

Location _____

Disposition contact _____

Tel W _____ ext _____ C_____

INSURANCE POLICIES
List your life, health, travel, mortgage and other insurance policies

Type _____ Policy Nº _____

Carrier _____

Contact _____ Tel _____

Type _____ Policy Nº _____

Carrier _____

Contact _____ Tel _____

Notes _____

_____

_____

INSURANCE POLICIES
List your life, health, travel, mortgage and other insurance policies

Type _____ Policy Nº _____

Carrier _____

Contact _____ Tel _____

Type _____ Policy Nº _____

Carrier _____

Contact _____ Tel _____

Type _____ Policy Nº _____

Carrier _____

Contact _____ Tel _____

MEMBERSHIP & LOYALTY CARDS
Example: Air Miles, Aeroplan, Optimum, CAA, AAA and others

Card 1 _____ Acct Nº _____

Contact _____ Tel _____

Card 2 _____ Acct Nº _____

Contact _____ Tel _____

Card 3 _____ Acct Nº _____

Contact _____ Tel _____

Card 4 _____ Acct Nº _____

Contact _____ Tel _____

Card 5 _____ Acct Nº _____

Contact _____ Tel _____

CAA - Canadian Automobile Association | **AAA** - American Automobile Association

MEMBERSHIP & LOYALTY CARDS   *Example: Air Miles, Aeroplan, Optimum, CAA, AAA and others*

Card 6 _____ Acct Nº _____

Contact _____ Tel _____

Card 7 _____ Acct Nº _____

Contact _____ Tel _____

Card 8 _____ Acct Nº _____

Contact _____ Tel _____

Card 9 _____ Acct Nº _____

Contact _____ Tel _____

Card 10 _____ Acct Nº _____

Contact _____ Tel _____

TRANSPORTATION CARDS
Example: Bus/metro, trains

Card 1 _____ Acct Nº _____

Contact _____ Tel _____

Card 2 _____ Acct Nº _____

Contact _____ Tel _____

Notes _____

_____

_____

_____

_____

LINE OF CREDIT
List your bank, credit card, or other line of credit

Bank_____Acct Nº _____

Contact_____Tel _____

Bank_____Acct Nº _____

Contact_____Tel _____

PERSONAL LOANS
List any outstanding loans other than mortgage

Type _____Acct Nº _____

Lender _____Tel _____

Type _____Acct Nº _____

Lender _____Tel _____

MAJOR CREDIT CARDS
Example: Visa, MasterCard, American Express and Discovery cards

Card 1 _____Card Nº_____

Contact_____Tel _____

Card 2 _____Card Nº_____

Contact_____Tel _____

Card 3 _____Card Nº_____

Contact_____Tel _____

STORE SPECIFIC CARDS
Example: Home Depot, Walmart, PC cards

Store 1_____Card Nº_____

Contact_____Tel _____

STORE SPECIFIC CARDS *Example: Home Depot, Walmart, PC cards*

Store 2_____Card Nº_____

Contact_____Tel _____

Store 3_____Card Nº_____

Contact_____Tel _____

INCOME TAX INSTALLMENTS

Revenu Quebec _____SIN _____

Contact_____Tel _____

Canada Revenue Agency _____SIN _____

Contact_____Tel _____

Internal Revenue Service (US) _____SSN_____

Contact_____Tel _____

State Revenue Department (US) _____SSN_____

Contact_____Tel _____

UTILITIES
List your regular utility bills

Electricity_____Company _____

Acct Nº _____ Contact_____Tel _____

Gas _____Company _____

Acct Nº _____ Contact_____Tel _____

Water _____Company _____

Acct Nº _____ Contact_____Tel _____

UTILITIES   *List your regular utility bills*

Heating oil _____ Company _____

Acct Nº _____ Tel _____

Other _____ Company _____

Acct Nº _____ Tel _____

HOUSING AND OTHER RENTED PROPERTIES
Rented primary and secondary housing

Rental 1 _____

Owner _____ Tel _____

Acct Nº _____ Contact _____ Tel _____

Rental 2 _____

Owner _____ Tel _____

Acct Nº _____ Contact _____ Tel _____

COMMUNICATION AND ENTERTAINMENT
List your providers for mobile phone, internet, cable, satellite and streaming services

Cell phone _____ Provider _____

Acct Nº _____ Tel _____

Internet _____ Provider _____

Acct Nº _____ Tel _____

Cable/Satellite _____ Provider _____

Acct Nº _____ Tel _____

Notes _____

_____

_____

COMMUNICATION & ENTERTAINMENT
List your cell phone, Internet, cable, satellite and streaming providers

Landline _____ Company _____

Acct Nº _____ Tel _____

Streaming _____ Company _____

Acct Nº _____ Tel _____

Other _____ Company _____

Acct Nº _____ Tel _____

SERVICES
List your cleaning, gardening, dog walking, snow removal services

Service _____ Company _____

Acct Nº _____ Contact _____ Tel _____

Service _____ Company _____

Acct Nº _____ Contact _____ Tel _____

Service _____ Company _____

Acct Nº _____ Contact _____ Tel _____

Notes _____

_____

_____

_____

_____

_____

_____

_____

DIGITAL FOOTPRINT

EQUIPMENT / HARDWARE
List all your computer and gadget hardware

Computer _____ Location _____

Login user ID _____ PW _____

Cell phone _____ Location _____

Login user ID _____ PW _____

Laptop _____ Location _____

Login user ID _____ PW _____

Smart watch _____ Location _____

Login user ID _____ PW _____

Tablet _____ Location _____

Login user ID _____ PW _____

Digital media player 1 _____ Location _____

Login user ID _____ PW _____

Digital media player 2 _____ Location _____

Login user ID _____ PW _____

E-Book reader _____ Location _____

Login user ID _____ PW _____

Notes _____

_____

_____

_____

WEBSITES   *List all your apps, website locations, and user info*

SITE/APP NAME_____

Web address (URL)_____

Login User ID_____ PW_____

Security **Q 1**_____ **A 1**_____

Security **Q 2**_____ **A 2**_____

Security **Q 3**_____ **A 3**_____

SITE/APP NAME_____

Web address (URL)_____

Login User ID_____ PW_____

Security **Q 1**_____ **A 1**_____

Security **Q 2**_____ **A 2**_____

Security **Q 3**_____ **A 3**_____

SITE/APP NAME_____

Web address (URL)_____

Login User ID_____ PW_____

Security **Q 1**_____ **A 1**_____

Security **Q 2**_____ **A 2**_____

Security **Q 3**_____ **A 3**_____

SITE/APP NAME_____

Web address (URL)_____

Login User ID_____ PW_____

Security **Q 1**_____ **A 1**_____

Security **Q 2**_____ **A 2**_____

Security **Q 3**_____ **A 3**_____

WEBSITES   *List all your apps, website locations, and user info*

SITE/APP NAME_____

Web address (URL)_____

Login User ID_____ PW_____

Security **Q 1**_____ **A 1**_____

Security **Q 2**_____ **A 2**_____

Security **Q 3**_____ **A 3**_____

SITE/APP NAME_____

Web address (URL)_____

Login User ID_____ PW_____

Security **Q 1**_____ **A 1**_____

Security **Q 2**_____ **A 2**_____

Security **Q 3**_____ **A 3**_____

SITE/APP NAME_____

Web address (URL)_____

Login User ID_____ PW_____

Security **Q 1**_____ **A 1**_____

Security **Q 2**_____ **A 2**_____

Security **Q 3**_____ **A 3**_____

SITE/APP NAME_____

Web address (URL)_____

Login User ID_____ PW_____

Security **Q 1**_____ **A 1**_____

Security **Q 2**_____ **A 2**_____

Security **Q 3**_____ **A 3**_____

WEBSITES *List all your apps, website locations, and user info*

SITE/APP NAME_____

Web address (URL)_____

Login User ID_____ PW_____

Security **Q 1**_____ **A 1**_____

Security **Q 2**_____ **A 2**_____

Security **Q 3**_____ **A 3**_____

SITE/APP NAME_____

Web address (URL)_____

Login User ID_____ PW_____

Security **Q 1**_____ **A 1**_____

Security **Q 2**_____ **A 2**_____

Security **Q 3**_____ **A 3**_____

SITE/APP NAME_____

Web address (URL)_____

Login User ID_____ PW_____

Security **Q 1**_____ **A 1**_____

Security **Q 2**_____ **A 2**_____

Security **Q 3**_____ **A 3**_____

SITE/APP NAME_____

Web address (URL)_____

Login User ID_____ PW_____

Security **Q 1**_____ **A 1**_____

Security **Q 2**_____ **A 2**_____

Security **Q 3**_____ **A 3**_____

WEBSITES *List all your apps, website locations, and user info*

SITE/APP NAME_____

Web address (URL)_____

Login User ID _____ PW_____

Security **Q 1**_____ **A 1**_____

Security **Q 2**_____ **A 2**_____

Security **Q 3**_____ **A 3**_____

SITE/APP NAME_____

Web address (URL)_____

Login User ID _____ PW_____

Security **Q 1**_____ **A 1**_____

Security **Q 2**_____ **A 2**_____

Security **Q 3**_____ **A 3**_____

SITE/APP NAME_____

Web address (URL)_____

Login User ID _____ PW_____

Security **Q 1**_____ **A 1**_____

Security **Q 2**_____ **A 2**_____

Security **Q 3**_____ **A 3**_____

SITE/APP NAME_____

Web address (URL)_____

Login User ID _____ PW_____

Security **Q 1**_____ **A 1**_____

Security **Q 2**_____ **A 2**_____

Security **Q 3**_____ **A 3**_____

WEBSITES *List all your apps, website locations, and user info*

SITE/APP NAME_____

Web address (URL)_____

Login User ID_____ PW_____

Security **Q 1**_____ **A 1**_____

Security **Q 2**_____ **A 2**_____

Security **Q 3**_____ **A 3**_____

SITE/APP NAME_____

Web address (URL)_____

Login User ID_____ PW_____

Security **Q 1**_____ **A 1**_____

Security **Q 2**_____ **A 2**_____

Security **Q 3**_____ **A 3**_____

SITE/APP NAME_____

Web address (URL)_____

Login User ID_____ PW_____

Security **Q 1**_____ **A 1**_____

Security **Q 2**_____ **A 2**_____

Security **Q 3**_____ **A 3**_____

SITE/APP NAME_____

Web address (URL)_____

Login User ID_____ PW_____

Security **Q 1**_____ **A 1**_____

Security **Q 2**_____ **A 2**_____

Security **Q 3**_____ **A 3**_____

WEBSITES   *List all your apps, website locations, and user info*

SITE/APP NAME_____

Web address (URL)_____

Login User ID _____ PW_____

Security **Q 1**_____ **A 1**_____

Security **Q 2**_____ **A 2**_____

Security **Q 3**_____ **A 3**_____

SITE/APP NAME_____

Web address (URL)_____

Login User ID _____ PW_____

Security **Q 1**_____ **A 1**_____

Security **Q 2**_____ **A 2**_____

Security **Q 3**_____ **A 3**_____

SITE/APP NAME_____

Web address (URL)_____

Login User ID _____ PW_____

Security **Q 1**_____ **A 1**_____

Security **Q 2**_____ **A 2**_____

Security **Q 3**_____ **A 3**_____

SITE/APP NAME_____

Web address (URL)_____

Login User ID _____ PW_____

Security **Q 1**_____ **A 1**_____

Security **Q 2**_____ **A 2**_____

Security **Q 3**_____ **A 3**_____

WEBSITES *List all your apps, website locations, and user info*

SITE/APP NAME_____

Web address (URL)_____

Login User ID_____ PW_____

Security **Q 1**_____ **A 1**_____

Security **Q 2**_____ **A 2**_____

Security **Q 3**_____ **A 3**_____

SITE/APP NAME_____

Web address (URL)_____

Login User ID_____ PW_____

Security **Q 1**_____ **A 1**_____

Security **Q 2**_____ **A 2**_____

Security **Q 3**_____ **A 3**_____

SITE/APP NAME_____

Web address (URL)_____

Login User ID_____ PW_____

Security **Q 1**_____ **A 1**_____

Security **Q 2**_____ **A 2**_____

Security **Q 3**_____ **A 3**_____

SITE/APP NAME_____

Web address (URL)_____

Login User ID_____ PW_____

Security **Q 1**_____ **A 1**_____

Security **Q 2**_____ **A 2**_____

Security **Q 3**_____ **A 3**_____

ITEMS WITH MONETARY VALUE
List your valuable possessions and note if this is gifted and to whom

Item _____ Location _____

Name _____ Gift (Y) _____ (N) _____

Contact _____ Tel _____

Item _____ Location _____

Name _____ Gift (Y) _____ (N) _____

Contact _____ Tel _____

Item _____ Location _____

Name _____ Gift (Y) _____ (N) _____

Contact _____ Tel _____

Item _____ Location _____

Name _____ Gift (Y) _____ (N) _____

Contact _____ Tel _____

WHERE/HOW TO SELL   *List your preferred method of sale*

Direct Sale _____ Evaluation _____

Sale by whom _____

Contact _____ Tel _____

Auction Sale _____ Evaluation _____

Auction house _____

Contact _____ Tel _____

Consignment _____ Evaluation _____

Store _____

Contact _____ Tel _____

ITEMS   *List your preferred method of sale or dispersal*

Collectible furniture _____

_____

_____

_____

_____

Art _____

_____

_____

_____

_____

Jewelry _____

_____

_____

_____

_____

Collectible books _____

_____

_____

_____

_____

ITEMS *List your preferred method of sale or dispersal*

Stamp/coin collection _____

_____

_____

_____

_____

_____

Designer clothing _____

_____

_____

_____

_____

_____

Saleable hobby projects _____

_____

_____

_____

_____

Notes_____

_____

_____

_____

_____

_____

_____

_____

NO MONETARY VALUE   *List your preferred method of dispersal or disposal: gift, donation, estate/garage sale, online marketplace sale, freecycle, trash*

Household furnishings _____

_____

_____

Clothing _____

_____

Costume jewelry _____

_____

Decor: paintings, knick-knacks _____

_____

_____

Books _____

_____

_____

Kitchen goods/appliances _____

_____

Electronics _____

_____

_____

Hobby projects/supplies _____

_____

_____

THIS SECTION LAST UPDATED: _____

FINAL PERSONAL
Details to be filled out by your executor when the time comes

Date of death _____

Place of death _____

Organ donation _____

FINAL RESTING ARRANGEMENTS
Your choice of burial, cremation, or other arrangements

Burial _____ **Cremation** _____ **Other** _____

Funeral home _____

Contact _____

Tel W _____ext_____C_____

E-mail 1 _____ 2 _____

Donation to science _____

Contact _____

Tel W _____ext_____C_____

E-mail 1 _____ 2 _____

Other _____

Type of arrangement _____

Contact _____

Tel W _____ext_____C_____

E-mail 1 _____ 2 _____

Notes _____

_____

_____

_____

_____

FUNERAL PROCEDURES
Special instructions for your final farewell

Officiant _____

_____

Eulogy_____

_____

Announcements _____

_____

Obituary _____

_____

Ceremony_____

_____

Music _____

_____

Presentation_____

_____

Donation direction_____

_____

Invitations _____

_____

Social gathering_____

_____

Particular wishes_____

_____

_____

_____

_____

_____

TO BE NOTIFIED AT DEATH
List your utility and other service accounts including automated transactions

Utilities _____ Acct N° _____

Contact _____ Tel _____

Utilities _____ Acct N° _____

Contact _____ Tel _____

Utilities _____ Acct N° _____

Contact _____ Tel _____

Utilities _____ Acct N° _____

Contact _____ Tel _____

Internet _____ Acct N° _____

Contact _____ Tel _____

Television _____ Acct N° _____

Contact _____ Tel _____

Cell phone _____ Acct N° _____

Contact _____ Tel _____

Landline _____ Acct N° _____

Contact _____ Tel _____

GOVERNMENT AGENCIES *List Service Canada and pension accounts*

Service Canada (OAS/GIS/CPP) _____ SIN _____

Tel _____ Website _____

Retraite Québec (QPP) _____

Tel _____ Website _____

Social Security (US) _____ SSN _____

Tel _____

OAS - Old Age Security I **GIS** - Guaranteed Income Supplement
CPP - Canada Pension Plan I **QPP** - Quebec Pension Plan

EXTRA PAGES *for the overflow from other lists or your own list categories*

EXTRA PAGES *for the overflow from other lists or your own list categories*

EXTRA PAGES *for the overflow from other lists or your own list categories*

EXTRA PAGES *for the overflow from other lists or your own list categories*

References

A great deal of estate settling information can be found online. The Canada Revenue Agency (CRA) has a list of links to online resources for each province https://tinyurl.com/mrrxv85c, as well as a general document detailing what needs to be done after death from their perspective. You should be able to find online lists of executor duties for your province, territory, or state. Each province also has online information. Links for each province can be found on the CRA site.

Each jurisdiction has its own peculiarities, and laws can change. References listed here may be out of date by the time you need to consult them. An online search for your part of the world is probably the easiest way to find the resources you need.

The Internal Revenue Service (IRS) in the United States has an extensive section on estate requirements at https://tinyurl.com/5tdukcbt.

This is a great place to start. Individual states also have their own information, though some are more detailed than others. A good resource to start looking for information in your state is at https://statelaws.findlaw.com/. You can look up your state and find available estate-related information. Not all states offer the same level of information.

Depending on the complexity of the estate you are dealing with, you may want to hire some help. A reputable estate lawyer (or a notary in Quebec) and a good accountant can go a long way towards making your process easier to manage. Your financial advisor may also be helpful. Once you have done your research as it pertains to your estate, you can add that information to the notebook for your representatives.

A Few Definitions

For clarification, here are explanations of a few of the terms used throughout this text:

Power of Attorney (POA) - A power of attorney is a legal document that you sign to give one or more persons the authority to manage your money and property on your behalf. In most of Canada, the person you appoint is called your attorney. Those named do not need to be lawyers.

Mandatary - In Quebec, the person who represents you when you have become incapacitated to the point where you can no longer act on your own behalf is your mandatary. In other jurisdictions the role has a different name, such as a healthcare or financial proxy.

Healthcare proxy - This is the person who makes healthcare decisions for you when you are no longer able to make those decisions for yourself.

Financial Proxy - This person will handle your financial affairs as per your authorization.

Executor (Liquidator in Quebec) - Your executor is the person or organization that handles the disposition of your estate once you have passed away.

Will/Codicil - Your will is the document that is processed after you die. In it you explicitly lay out what you want to happen to your goods and your money. A codicil is an addendum to a will that either adds to the provisions of the will or explicitly changes certain parameters of the original will. If there is a codicil, you will need both the will and the codicil to proceed with settling an estate.

Notary - In Quebec, a Notary is a lawyer who specializes in wills and estates, real estate, and contracts. In other jurisdictions you would most likely use a lawyer. In the United States a Notary Public is someone who can witness signatures or validate documents. In Canada that role is filled by a Commissioner of Oaths.

Acknowledgements/Gratitude

This guide, though short, is the culmination of many hours of work and input from numerous professionals and resources. I owe an enormous debt of gratitude to Susan Nichol of Nichol Services. She deals with other people's stuff for a living and she has provided me with the push to get moving, not only with this guide, but with seminars we offer that walk you through the necessary thought processes for old age planning. I am also grateful to the clients I retired from serving at the end of 2018, many of whom remain friends. They taught me a great deal about the variety of ways we manage our financial and health issues. Working with them gave me perspectives on these issues that I would not have reached without their input. Thank you also to Carol Adamakos, who did me the honour of taking over my practice, which freed me to work on this project.

I am very grateful to Wendy Moenig, designer and collaborator, for her enormous contribution to this project — part of the content of the book, the playful title, her wonderful illustrations (without which the book would not have taken shape), and her very personal and expressive designs for the logo and business cards for catherinerahal.com. To Joachim Moenig, thank you for reading my drafts, making constructive comments and keeping me focused on what is important.

Thanks go as well to Judy Mackintosh, Diana Bruno, Krista Brecht, Dorothy Azouz, Arthur Pereira, Dan Solomon, and Linde Howe-Beck for reading and giving me feedback on how the material comes across, providing comments about flow and content. Further gratitude goes to Ellie Presner, who provided the first round of proofreading. I am indebted to Brian Bradley and to Frederik Ehlen, each of whom provided additional rounds of proofreading that helped us enormously in polishing the final version.

Posthumous thanks go to Mohieddine Abdelkader Rahal, my late brother-in-law, who died far too young. He knew he was gravely ill and prepared for his wife a notebook that contained essential information she would need to settle his estate and to continue running the household. The memory of that notebook was a significant factor in motivating me to write this guide.

I am further indebted to Ross Whitaker, who took on the role of repeatedly reading my text and giving me additional perspective, both as to construction and content, as I came to the final redrafts.

To my beloved brother, Peter Schmitt, thank you for always being a loving and supportive sibling — you made the work of cleaning out our family home much easier than it might have been. We had agreed ages ago that we would never fight over "stuff" or money, and we made it work. Not a cross word between us during a very stressful time.

I also want to acknowledge the huge place in my life occupied by my loving and caring daughter-in-law, Cindy, and the two girls who have brought so much joy to my heart, my granddaughters Leela and Aubry.

The most important acknowledgement is to my much loved sons Jamal and Hakim — it is for you that I am preparing my own roadmap. The death of your father at age 37, far too early in his life and ours, was a defining event for us. You were too young then to understand the enormity of the difficulties that ensued. The day will come when the two of you will have to deal with my structured mess — I hope that this will help.